Dear God,

Imagine... the poor moon has to stay awake while the whole world sleeps

Annie

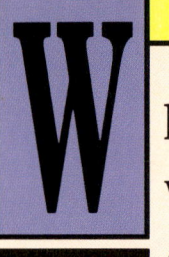

What should I be
when I grow up?
A captain on a cruise?
A builder, teacher,
doctor, clerk?
Please help me, God,
to choose.

Dear God,
...Do you have a job for me?

There are so many
things to learn.
I never can be bored.
Like, how do birds
begin to fly?
How did you
teach them, Lord?

Dear God,

...did you teach them how to build good nests?

Do people live in outer space?
And do they look like me?
I think I'll be an astronaut
and go up there to see.

Dear God,

...Do stars ever crash into one another, like us sometimes?

Annie

They say the world is round,
Dear God,
a ball up in the sky.
How come the people
don't fall off?
I know they don't, but *why?*

Dear God,
...what holds me up...when the world's upside down?

Annie

I wonder where you live,
Dear God—
I guess in every place.
You're in my heart
and in my house
and far away in space.

Dear God,

...I just can't find your place on the map

— Annie

Some flowers grow in summertime
and some in spring and fall.
You make them different, every one.
How do you do it all?

Dear God,
How do you tell all the flowers when to bloom?

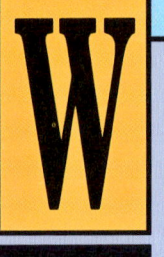

What's over there,
behind those hills?
I'd like to go and see.
But if I go and take a look
I know *you'll* be with me.

Dear God,
how can you
be here and there
...and there
...and here
and here
...there
...and ??

— Annie

10-1871